# Roots
of the **Blues**

by Peggy Bresnick Kendler

Editorial Offices: Glenview, Illinois • Parsippany, New Jersey • New York, New York
Sales Offices: Needham, Massachusetts • Duluth, Georgia • Glenview, Illinois
Coppell, Texas • Ontario, California • Mesa, Arizona

ISBN: 0-328-13541-0

3 4 5 6 7 8 9 10 V0G1 14 13 12 11 10 09 08 07 06

West African Music

The blues is a style of music. It has been popular in the United States since its invention in the early 1900s. Its roots go back to the music of West Africa.

Music has always been important to the many cultures of West Africa. It is a part of life for even the youngest West African child. For centuries, West Africans have made music in many ways for all sorts of occasions.

In West Africa, music or dance is a part of many activities, such as working, playing, and celebrating. Songs are often sung accompanied by drums, or with stringed musical instruments similar to the guitar and banjo.

Blues has its roots in West African music.

West African Musical Traditions

West African music is unique. It combines sounds from nature with spoken words. Each sound and song has its own unique meaning to the African people.

People called *griots* played an important role in West African music. Griots were musical entertainers. They played instruments that looked and sounded similar to a banjo.

The griots traveled from village to village playing music, telling jokes and stories, and giving advice. They knew about the history of each village and explained it through songs and stories. People came to **appreciate** them for the advice and entertainment that they offered.

A West African banjo (left) and a North American banjo (right)

The music that would become the blues developed among enslaved African Americans.

Coming to America

The English colony of Virginia was started in 1607. The first shipment of enslaved people arrived in 1619. This date marks the true beginning of the history of the blues.

The enslaved people were West Africans. They had been captured from their villages and forced onto ships bound for the Americas. Once the West Africans arrived, plantation owners purchased them from the people who brought them over. The West Africans were given just food, water, and shelter, but they were not paid for their work. And they were not free to leave. Living in **slavery** was very hard.

A Life of Slavery

Between 1619 and 1808, millions of enslaved West Africans were brought by ship to the Americas. Among them were West Africans who had once been griots. Instead of telling jokes and stories as they would have back in West Africa, these former griots sang songs that told of their unhappiness and expressed their fear that they would never see their homes again.

Most enslaved people did farm labor on plantations. They often sang work songs while working in the fields.

These songs often focused on their sadness. But they also kept the enslaved West Africans' spirits up as they worked. Enslaved people managed to preserve the unique West African musical style through their work songs.

While laboring in the fields, they used a West African musical technique called *call-and-response*. The song leader would call out a sentence or phrase. Then the other people would sing with an answering sentence or phrase, as a **choir** in a church might do.

Call-and-response was a kind of musical conversation. One person led, and the others followed. The enslaved people also sang *field hollers*. These were long, drawn-out cries sung over long distances, from one field to the next.

A modern choir

Early African Americans sang spirituals, songs that reflected their hopes for the future.

Religion Shapes Music

Many of the enslaved West Africans were introduced to Christianity after they were brought to the Americas. They continued to celebrate their own West African traditions, but they also practiced some parts of Christianity. The parts that spoke about freedom from suffering were especially popular.

The plantation owners forbade their enslaved workers from meeting in groups, so they met secretly. During those secret meetings they prayed, danced, and spoke of their own personal experiences. They also sang a type of song called a *spiritual.*

Spirituals were both **religious** and full of emotion. They expressed the enslaved West Africans' feelings and hopes for the future. Spirituals played an important role in the development of blues music.

The Blues Comes of Age

No one knows where the first blues song was performed, or who sang or wrote it. What we do know, however, is that blues music sprang up in different parts of the American South during the 1890s.

Early blues music was inspired by call-and-response, field hollers, and spirituals. The earliest blues singers played handmade musical instruments, which made interesting and unusual sounds.

The Roots of Blues Music

1912 An early blues song, W. C. Handy's "Memphis Blues" is published.

1914 W. C. Handy's "St. Louis Blues" is published.

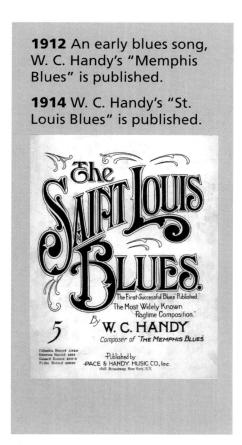

1920 Mamie Smith records "Crazy Blues."

Among these early instruments were the handmade banjo, and the washboard and stick. Later on, blues musicians would play guitars, pianos, and harmonicas. Blues musicians became known for experimenting with different sounds.

Early blues music was usually played by roaming musicians who were similar to the griots. Their audiences were mostly farm workers who would take breaks from their work and dance to the music.

1923 Bessie Smith records "Down Hearted Blues." Gertrude "Ma" Rainey records "New Boweavil Blues." The recordings help make blues popular throughout the United States.

1925–1929 "Blind Lemon" Jefferson records nearly one hundred blues songs.

1930s Different types of blues music begin to appear in different areas, such as the Mississippi delta and Memphis, Tennessee.

Early blues musician W. C. Handy is sometimes called "the Father of the Blues."

Early Blues Musicians

In 1903, W. C. Handy heard a man in the Tutwiler, Mississippi, train station playing the guitar. The man slid a pocket knife up and down the guitar, making an unusual sound.

What Handy heard was an early form of the slide guitar blues. Later, he wrote down the notes. Blues historians believe this was the first time that blues music was written down.

Handy later gained fame as a bandleader, songwriter, and performer. He published "Memphis Blues," an early blues song, in 1912.

Mamie Smith was a stage singer and the first person to record a blues song. Smith recorded "Crazy Blues" in 1920. Smith inspired other female singers to record blues music.

"Blind Lemon" Jefferson was a singer, musician, and songwriter. Jefferson, who was blind since childhood, recorded nearly one hundred blues songs from 1925 to 1929.

Bessie Smith was an early blues singer. She wrote many blues songs, including the hit, "Back Water Blues." She also influenced many future female blues singers.

Gertrude "Ma" Rainey is sometimes called "the Mother of the Blues." She began singing blues on stage in 1904 and recorded blues music in 1923.

Different Places, Different Styles

Slavery was abolished in 1865. Formerly enslaved people were **released** to settle anywhere in the country. Different styles of blues were created as they moved around.

The Memphis Blues, which originated in Memphis, Tennessee, featured one guitarist playing rhythm guitar and another one playing lead guitar. The East Texas Blues sounded like old work songs. It used guitar or piano for rhythm. The Piedmont Blues, from North Carolina, was influenced by ragtime, a form of jazz music. It was more melodic than other blues styles.

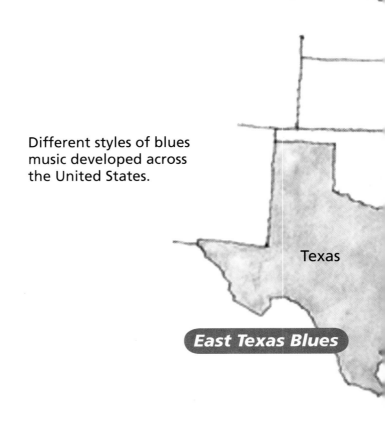

Different styles of blues music developed across the United States.

Texas

East Texas Blues

The Delta Blues began among African Americans of the Mississippi Delta. It blended work songs and field hollers with musicians playing slide guitars and harmonicas. In Chicago, blues musicians added electric guitar and drums to the Delta Blues style. Their music became known as Chicago Blues.

Chicago Blues

Illinois

West Virginia

Virginia

Memphis Blues

Piedmont Blues

North Carolina

Delta Blues

South Carolina

Georgia

Tennessee

Louisiana

Mississippi

Arkansas

Modern Blues Greats

There have been hundreds of great blues musicians since the early 1900s. Millions of listeners have enjoyed their music.

The most famous blues musicians each have their own style and talent. For example, Bo Diddley's soul music influenced rock and roll. Billie Holiday was a world-famous female vocalist. Her soulful style of singing the blues was unique and personalized. John Lee Hooker's growling voice blended with one repeating musical chord for a special blues style.

Muddy Waters

Bo Diddley

B. B. King, who grew up in Mississippi and lived in Memphis, Tennessee, as a **teenager** and young man, has been called "the King of the Blues." King often picks at a single guitar string to produce many different emotional sounds. As a boy, Muddy Waters worked in the cotton fields of the Mississippi delta. In the early 1940s, he moved to Chicago to play the blues. Waters eventually became one of the great Chicago Blues musicians.

John Lee Hooker

Billie Holiday

B. B. King

The blues is related to many forms of popular music, including the jazz that is being played by these musicians.

The Blues and Its Relatives

Blues music has had a major influence on today's popular music. You can find elements of the blues in most of the modern popular music styles, including jazz, rock, rap, and soul.

Buddy Bolden formed one of the first jazz bands in 1895. Buddy, who may have started out working as a **barber,** played the cornet, an instrument similar to a bugle or trumpet. His jazz music sounded a great deal like the blues music of the time.

One of today's popular musical styles, rap, comes from the same roots as the blues. Rap has rhyming lyrics. The lyrics are spoken rhythmically while musical instruments are played. Rap music often tells stories in a style similar to that used by the griots.

Without the blues, American music would be very different from what it is today. From its quiet beginnings, the blues has become a major part of American life!

Glossary

appreciate *v.* to think highly of; to recognize the worth or quality of; value; enjoy

barber *n.* a person whose business is cutting hair and shaving or trimming beards

choir *n.* a group of singers who sing together, often in a church service

released *v.* let go, freed, unlatched

religious *adj.* much interested in the belief, study, and worship of God or gods; devoted to religion

slavery *n.* the condition of being owned by another person and being made to work without wages

teenager *n.* a person between the ages of thirteen and nineteen